Animal Classifications

Mammals

Angela Royston

raintree

a Capstone company — publishers for children

Edited by Helen Cox Cannons, Clare Lewis and
    Abby Colich
Designed by Steve Mead
Picture research by Tracy Cummins
Production by Victoria Fitzgerald
Originated by Capstone Global Library Ltd
Printed and bound in China

ISBN 978 1 406 28740 0
18 17 16 15 14
10 9 8 7 6 5 4 3 2 1

British Library Cataloguing in Publication Data
A full catalogue record for this book is available from the British Library.

Acknowledgements
We would like to thank the following for permission to reproduce photographs: Capstone Press: Karon Dubke, 27; Getty Images: Dr Clive Bromhall, 25, Mark Carwardine, 13, 29 Top; Shutterstock: Anan Kaewkhammul, Design Element, Bailey0ne, 4, CanuckStock, 19, Christopher Elwell, 23, Four Oaks, 15, glenda, 18, Ivan Kuzmin, 7, Jarry, 20, 29 Bottom, Ken Wolter, 12, Kirsanov Valeriy Vladimirovich, 21, lightpoet, 11, Cover, Monkey Business Images, 26, Oleg Znamenskiy, 6, Seleznev Oleg, 8, 29 Middle, Stuart G Porter, 10, T.W. van Urk, 5, worldswildlifewonders, 17; SuperStock: Minden Pictures, 14; Thinkstock: Alan Jeffery, 24, Andre Anita, 9, Jiri Haureljuk, 16, 28, Photoservice, 22.

We would like to thank Michael Bright for his invaluable help in the preparation of this book.

Contents

Some words are shown in bold, **like this**. You can find out what they mean by looking in the glossary.

Meet the mammals

Dogs, squirrels, sheep and elephants are all mammals. Mammals are animals that have hair on their bodies and that feed their babies with milk from the mother.

Dogs and humans have lots of hair, so they are **classified** as mammals.

Two lambs feed on milk, which they suck from the mother sheep.

Scientists sort living things into groups. This is called **classification**. Each group of living things is different from other groups in particular ways.

Body shape

Mammals are part of a bigger group called **vertebrates**. This group also includes **reptiles** and birds. All vertebrates have a backbone and a hard **skeleton** inside their bodies. The skeleton gives their body its shape.

Giraffes have the longest legs and longest neck of any mammal.

bones in wings

legs

Bats are the only mammals that have wings.

Most mammals have four legs, or two legs and two arms. Bats are mammals, but they have two legs and two wings. The wings are made of long, thin finger bones, with skin stretched between them.

Hair and fur

A mammal has hair that grows from its skin. Hair protects the skin and helps to keep the mammal warm. Some mammals, such as wolves, have thick hair. Others, such as elephants, have only a few hairs.

A camel's hair protects its skin from the hot sun.

A polar bear lives in the icy Arctic. Its thick hair helps to keep it warm.

Mammals are **warm blooded**, which means that they make heat using the energy from food. Blood carries the heat all around their bodies.

Cats

Mammals are **classified** into smaller groups and **families**. The cat family includes big cats, such as lions, cheetahs and tigers, as well as smaller pet cats. All cats look similar. For example, they have long backs and most have long tails.

A cheetah bends its long back as it runs.

It is easy to see that a lynx is a type of cat.

Cats have sharp claws and sharp teeth. They need them because they are **carnivores**. Carnivores eat meat from other animals.

Sea mammals

Sea mammals, including seals, dolphins and whales, live in the sea. Seals have thick fur, but most sea mammals, such as walruses and whales, have almost no hair.

Seals spend some time on land but they hunt for food in the sea.

The blue whale is the largest animal that has ever lived.

Instead of legs and arms, sea mammals have **flippers**, which they use to swim. Unlike fish, sea mammals cannot breathe in water. They have to come to the surface to breathe.

Giving birth

Instead of laying eggs, almost all mammals give birth to babies. The babies are small, but have the same body shape as their parents. Some mammals have several babies at a time. Others have one or two.

This dog has six puppies, which all look like her.

An elephant usually has one baby calf at a time.

All mammal mothers make milk in special parts of their body called **mammary glands**. Babies feed on their mother's milk until they are old enough to eat other food.

Marsupials

Kangaroos and koalas are both **marsupials**. Female marsupials have a special **pouch**. A baby marsupial is born when it is still tiny and not fully formed. It crawls into its mother's pouch, where it feeds on milk and grows bigger.

A kangaroo baby is safe in its mother's pouch.

Young koalas stay close to their mothers even after they have left the pouch.

A baby marsupial is called a joey. When the joey is big enough, it leaves the pouch and explores the world.

Looking after young

Mammals take care of their young until they are old enough to look after themselves. Baby mammals stay close to their mothers, who try to keep them safe from **predators**.

Newborn deer can stand and walk when they are only a few hours old.

A tiger cub practises stalking. It moves forward slowly then pounces.

Baby mammals learn many skills from their mothers. For example, tiger cubs learn how to hunt for food.

Rodents

Mice, hamsters, squirrels and prairie dogs all belong to a group of mammals called **rodents**. Many female rodents have lots of babies at the same time. A group of babies is called a **litter**.

All rodents have four large front teeth and gnaw their food.

A house mouse can have many litters of babies every year.

Baby rodents grow up fast! A house mouse starts to have her own babies when she is just two months old. She may produce 150 babies a year!

Herds and packs

Mammals that feed on plants, such as zebra and buffalo, live in large groups called **herds**. Living in a group makes it easier for these animals to stay safe from **predators**. Some mammal predators hunt together in groups called packs.

These zebras watch out for danger as they graze on the grass.

Prairie dogs leave their underground homes to feed.

Smaller mammals, such as **rodents** and rabbits, **burrow** under the ground. For example, prairie dogs live together in vast underground "towns".

Monkeys and apes

Monkeys, lemurs and apes belong to a group of mammals called **primates**. Monkeys mostly live high among the trees. They leap from branch to branch and tree to tree.

Some monkeys use their tail like an extra arm or leg to grip onto a branch.

A chimpanzee uses a rock as a tool to crack open nuts.

Apes include humans, so other apes are more like us than other animals. Apes have no tail and can stand on their two back legs.

One amazing mammal!

Humans are perhaps the most amazing mammal. Humans can speak, read and write. They can compose music and invent complicated machines. They can discuss ideas and plan for the future.

Human children take many years to grow up because they have so much to learn!

Humans love and care for other animals. This girl looks after her pet cat.

Humans understand the world better than any other animal. Can we use that understanding to make the world a better place for all animals to live in?

Quiz

Look at the pictures below and read the clues. Can you remember the names of these mammals? Look back in the book if you need help.

1. I am safe inside my mother's **pouch**. What am I?

Answers
1. joey
2. whale
3. camel
4. squirrel

2. I live in the sea but I breathe in air. What am I?

3. I live in the desert. My hair protects me from the sun. What am I?

4. I am a **rodent** I have four large front teeth. What am I?

Glossary

burrow animal's underground home; digging an underground home

carnivore animal that eats other animals for food

classification system that scientists use to divide living things into separate groups

classified put into a group according to special things shared by that group

flipper hard, flat part of a sea mammal's body, which it uses to swim

herd large group of animals

litter number of babies born at the same time

mammary gland part of a female mammal's body that can make milk

marsupial mammal that gives birth to young that are not fully formed and continue to grow in the mother's pouch

pouch pocket-like body part on the outside of the body

predator animal that kills other animals for food

primate member of a group of mammals that have hands and hand-like feet. Monkeys, apes and humans are primates.

reptile member of a group of animals that have a dry, scaly skin

rodent member of a group of mammals that have four large front teeth, which they use to gnaw food

vertebrate animal that has a backbone and skeleton inside its body

warm blooded able to make body heat from food

Find out more

Books

Mammals (Deadly Factbook), Steve Backshall (Orion Books, 2012)

Mammals (True or False), Melvin and Gilda Berger (Scholastic, 2011)

RSPB First Book of Mammals, Anita Ganeri and David Chandler (A & C Black, 2011)

Whales and Dolphins (Mad About), Anita Ganeri (Ladybird, 2009)

Why do Mammals Have Fur?, Pat Jacobs (Franklin Watts, 2014)

Websites

kids.sandiegozoo.org/animals/mammals

The kids' section of the San Diego Zoo website includes photos and information about mammals. Click the small photos to find out about particular animals. Don't miss the games, videos and animal cams at the top.

www.nhm.ac.uk/kids-only

The "kids only" section of the Natural History Museum website includes the blue whale and the giant sloth, two of the stars of the museum.

Index

Life in a Pack

Wolves

Richard and Louise Spilsbury

www.heinemann.co.uk/library

To order:
☎ Phone 44 (0) 1865 888066
🖹 Send a fax to 44 (0) 1865 314091
💻 Visit the Heinemann Bookshop at www.heinemann.co.uk/library to browse our catalogue and order online.

First published in Great Britain by Heinemann Library, Halley Court, Jordan Hill, Oxford OX2 8EJ, part of Harcourt Education.
Heinemann is a registered trademark of Harcourt Education Ltd.

© Harcourt Education Ltd 2003
The moral right of the proprietor has been asserted.

Editorial: Nicole Irving and Georga Godwin
Design: Ron Kamen and Celia Floyd
Picture Research: Catherine Bevan and Charlotte Lippmann
Production: Lorraine Warner

Originated by Dot Gradations Ltd
Printed in Hong Kong, China by Wing King Tong

ISBN 0 431 16924 1 (hardback)
08 07 06 05 04
10 9 8 7 6 5 4 3 2 1

British Library Cataloguing in Publication Data

Spilsbury, Richard and Spilsbury, Louise
Animal Groups: Wolves – Life in a pack
599.7'73'156
A full catalogue record for this book is available from the British Library.

Acknowledgements

The publishers would like to thank the following for permission to reproduce photographs:
Bruce Coleman Collection p28, /Staffan Widstrand p23, /Uwe Walz p6; Corbis pp24, 25; FLPA/Gerard Lacz pp4, 11, 17, 18, /Mark Newman p5, /Minden Pictures pp14, 15, 19, /Terry Whittaker p10; Nature Picture Library/Nigel Bean p9; NHPA/T Kitchin and V Hurst pp7, 12, 20; Oxford Scientific Films/Daniel Cox pp13, 16, /Lon E Lauber p22, /Marty Stouffer Prods/AA p26; www.wolfpaper/pl/photos Monty Sloan p21.

Cover photograph of an European grey wolf, reproduced with permission of NHPA/Gerard Lacz.

Contents

Any words appearing in the text in bold, **like this**, are explained in the Glossary.

Wolves are large, wild dogs. They have long legs, big feet and a long, bushy tail. Most have a coat of thick hair on their bodies. Adult **male** wolves are 1.5 to 2 metres long from the tip of the nose to the end of the tail. That is about as long as an average adult person is tall. Male wolves are about 75 centimetres tall. **Female** wolves look very similar, but they are a little smaller.

Species of wolf

There are two species of wolf – the grey wolf and the red wolf. Grey wolves are larger and, despite their name, not always grey! Most are grey to greyish brown, sometimes with reddish fur on the neck, or patches of a different colour. Others may be completely black, cream or even white. Red wolves have shorter, redder hair. Both red and grey wolves are **endangered species**. Most do not live in the wild any more, but in special areas protected by people.

Most of the world's wolves are grey wolves, like this one. They look rather like German shepherd dogs, but they are more powerful. For example, their jaws are twice as strong!

What are dogs?

Wolves are members of the dog family. This includes **species** (kinds) such as foxes, jackals, coyotes and the dogs we keep as pets.

There are very few red wolves, like these, left in the world. Most live in parts of the south-eastern USA.

Groups of wolves

Although each wolf does some things alone, wolves are **social** animals and spend most of their time doing things with other wolves in a group. A group of wolves is called a pack. In this book we will look at how packs of grey wolves live together in the wild.

What is a wolf pack like?

A wolf pack is basically a family group. Most packs contain two parents and their young. Some packs also include a brother or sister of one of the parent wolves – an aunt or uncle to the youngsters. Every wolf has a particular **rank** or place in the pack. Wolves know who is above them and who is below them in rank.

Who's who in the pack?

The two parent wolves are called the **alpha** pair. They are the **dominant** or top-ranking wolves in the pack. The other wolves show respect to them and often do what they want. Although the alpha **male** and alpha **female** usually decide what the pack does, such as choosing where to sleep and when to hunt, they do not always tell the others what to do.

Most packs have around seven members, but some people have seen packs of up to 36 wolves!

The next most important are the **beta** wolves. These are usually wolves aged between one and three years old. The older beta wolves are higher up than the youngest beta wolves. The pups – wolves that are one-year-old or younger – come below their older brothers and sisters and the alpha wolves. The pups have their own ranking order that they work out while they play.

Knowing your place

You can usually tell which is the dominant wolf when any two wolves meet. The dominant wolf stands up tall, with its tail up, ears pointing forward and looks directly at the other wolf. The lower-ranking wolf crouches down, tucks its tail between its legs, holds its ears flat and looks away from the dominant wolf.

A dominant wolf and a lower-ranking wolf show their rank almost every time they meet.

Wolves can live in a wide variety of different places. They need what any other animal needs from a **habitat** – a supply of food, water to drink and a safe place to have young. Wolves prefer areas with some cover for them to rest or hide in, such as bushes or trees. They also avoid people as much as they can, so they tend to live in wilderness areas such as hills, forests or prairie (open land with tall grasses).

Around the world

Long ago, wolves lived all over the northern half of the world. Today, grey wolves live mainly in wild parts of North America, Asia, the Middle East and a few parts of Europe.

This white wolf is a kind of grey wolf that lives on Arctic tundra – land that is covered with ice and snow most of the year. Its white hair **camouflages** it against the snow.

8

What is a territory?

Each pack of wolves usually stays in a particular area, called its **territory**. This is the area in which they hunt, rest, sleep, play and raise pups. A pack tries to stop wolves from other packs going into their territory. Some packs have large territories; others have smaller territories. The size of a territory depends on the amount of food that is available in it.

Spring and summer territories

In spring and summer, a pack's territory is relatively small. At this time of the year, food is plentiful. Most animals have their young now, so there are more **prey** animals about. Young prey are also easier to catch. This is also the time when wolves have their young, and they never travel far from where the pups are kept.

In North America, caribou (reindeer) spend summer on the tundra, but travel hundreds of kilometres south to forests in winter. The wolves that feed on the caribou follow them all the way.

9

Autumn and winter territories

In winter, food is harder to find. Some prey animals **migrate**, others may **hibernate** and some are killed by the cold. The young prey are older now and faster so they are not so easy to catch. The pack has to travel much further to find prey and does not usually return to the same spot each day.

Scent marking territories

While people build walls or fences to stop others walking on their property, wolves use different ways to keep other packs out. They mark their territory by spraying a small amount of urine (wee) on raised objects, such as trees, rocks or bushes. These **scent marks** warn other wolf packs to 'keep out'.

When wolves smell a scent mark, they can tell if it was made by a wolf from their own pack or by a stranger.

What do wolves eat?

Wolves are carnivores – animals that eat meat. Wolves mainly eat large animals, such as deer, moose, caribou and bison, because large animals provide them with lots of food. Wolves also eat smaller **prey** such as beavers, rabbits, squirrels and even fish! When they cannot find live prey, wolves will feed on **carrion** (dead animals) that may have been killed by other animals, or died from injury or old age.

The only way wolves can catch animals that are larger and stronger than themselves is to hunt in groups, working together to bring down the prey. This is one of the main reasons that wolves live in packs.

A wolf has 42 teeth. The long canines at the front – the fangs – are sharp and curved for gripping prey tightly. Wolves use their other teeth to bite through flesh and bone and grind their food.

11

A wolf's larder

If the pack catches several large animals within a few days, they may not be able to eat all the meat in one go. Instead, they bury leftovers in an underground store, called a cache, to eat later.

How much do they eat?

As soon as the wolves have caught an animal, they start to eat. Wolves usually go on eating until there is nothing left of the prey except the hooves and the biggest bones. Adult wolves can eat as much as 14 kilograms at once. This is not greed – it may be days before the pack catches another meal, so they have to eat as much as they can, when they can.

These wolves have killed a whitetail deer. They will hide any leftover meat by burying it to eat later, if **scavengers** don't find it first.

How do wolves hunt together?

Wolves usually hunt with their pack. When hunting, a wolf pack works as a team. Members of the team have different jobs to do and the **alpha** wolf usually tells them what to do and when to do it. When they set out on a hunt, the wolves travel in single file. When they find **prey**, they usually **stalk** it (sneak up on it) first. They move silently through the undergrowth, until they are close enough to break into a run and attack.

Locating prey

Wolves find prey by coming across it by chance, smelling it from a distance or following **scent trails** on the ground. Wolves have an excellent sense of smell and can detect prey from over 2 kilometres (about a mile) away!

Wolves mostly hunt at night, although they may hunt during the day in cold winters.

Fast on their feet

Wolves usually trot at about 8 kilometres (5 miles) an hour, but when chasing prey they can run up to 70 kilometres (45 miles) an hour.

Hunting tactics

Wolves use various hunting tactics. One or two wolves may chase a prey animal towards the rest of the pack. Sometimes the pack splits into two teams. The first chases the prey for a while, then the second takes over. This means they can keep chasing the prey until it is worn out.

A pack may chase a herd eight or nine times before they catch anything. Some scientists think this happens because the wolves are checking out the herd, to see which is the weakest and easiest animal to catch, before moving in for the kill.

These Arctic wolves are chasing a herd of musk oxen. They aim for the weakest herd member.

How do wolves care for their young?

The **alpha** pair in a pack usually stay together for life. Each year they **mate** and have a new **litter** (set) of baby wolves, called pups.

The alpha **male** and **female** mate in late winter to early spring, depending on where the pack lives. The new wolf pups are born about two months later. There are usually four to six pups in a litter.

Wolf pups

All wolf pups are born with dark fur and blue eyes. As they grow, their eyes become yellow-gold or orange. The colour of their fur changes, too. Even Arctic wolves, which have white hair as adults, are born with dark fur.

The pups are born in a **den**, which may be a cave, a hollow log, but most often in a hole underground. A den is usually near a river or lake, so that the mother does not have to go far to get water.

The pups' first weeks

The pups are born helpless, and their eyes and ears do not open until they are two weeks old. They begin to **suckle** (drink milk) from their mother straightaway. She stays in the den, which is often deep in the ground, caring for the pups until they can walk when they are three or four weeks old.

While the mother wolf is in the den with the pups, the other wolves hunt and bring food for her to eat.

When do pups leave the den?

The pups first leave the den when they are about a month old. The other wolves in the pack gather round to meet the pups as they come out. They all lick each other and wag their tails in excitement.

The whole pack helps to look after the pups when they are out of the den. Each wolf watches out for eagles, bears and other **predators**, which may attack a pup, and they all do their best to protect the pups. As well as looking after them, all the wolves in a pack seem to be very fond of the pups.

In play, the pups nip the ears and tails of the adults and jump and climb on them. The adults are very patient, but tell the pups off by baring their teeth if they get too rough.

Who feeds the pups?

Soon the pups are ready to start eating some meat. They cannot hunt yet, so the other wolves bring food to them. The adults eat a lot of meat after a successful hunt. When they return, they feed the pups. To tell an adult he or she is hungry, a pup licks the wolf's mouth. The adult regurgitates (spits up) some chewed meat for the pup to eat.

Play time!

Pups play together like many young animals, including children! They chase their own tails or pounce on twigs or stones. They also play with each other a lot, wrestling, chasing and play-fighting. Play helps them practise skills they will need when they are older, such as judging distance for pouncing and reacting quickly.

When pups play-fight, they often work out a **rank** order among themselves, which changes frequently. This helps them to understand how the rank system in the pack works.

Rendez-vous sites

When the pups are about two months old, the pack moves them to an open area, known as a rendez-vous site. *'Rendez-vous'* is the French for 'meeting', and this is where the pack meets. The pups stay here all the time and the adults return here after hunting.

Learning from others

When the pups are about three months old, they start to go along on some hunts. They watch the adults to learn what to do, what to catch and how to follow **scent trails**. By winter, the young wolves are able to travel and hunt along with the rest of the pack.

When the adults in a pack are out hunting, a low-ranking wolf usually stays behind to babysit the pups.

19

How do wolves communicate?

Wolves **communicate** (tell each other things) in lots of different ways. They make many sounds, including whimpers, growls, barks, whines and pants, which mean diffcrent things. For example, a growl means a wolf is not happy and a whimper says it is scared or hurt. Adult wolves hardly ever bark, although pups may bark when they are playing or to call for help.

Howling

A wolf's most famous sound is the howl. A wolf usually howls alone to find the rest of its pack, or to attract a **mate**. When wolves howl together they may be telling other wolf packs to keep away, helping the pack to feel like a team before going on a hunt, or just howling for the fun of it!

To tell other wolves that it is **dominant**, a wolf growls, like the wolf shown here. To answer that they know they are lower in the **rank** order, the other wolves whine.

20

Many pictures of wolves show them howling in front of the moon. In fact, wolves may howl at any time of the day or night. When a wolf pack howls together, other wolves can hear the sound up to 16 kilometres (10 miles) away.

Body language

Wolves also use parts of their body to say other things, as well as their rank in the pack. A pup asks to play by bowing down with its rear in the air, tail wagging. Wolves can also say a lot using just their ears! If a wolf is too near a dominant wolf's food, it apologizes and shows it knows its place by flattening its ears. If a wolf is cross, it points its ears forward towards the other wolf.

Communicating by smell

When wolves mark their **territories** with urine, they are using scent to communicate. When a wolf smells a **scent mark** like this, it can tell whether the wolf that left it is part of its own pack or an outsider, how old it is and even whether it is **male** or **female**!

A wolf often says 'hello' by licking another wolf's **muzzle** (nose and mouth). To greet an **alpha** wolf, a lower-ranking one nips at the centre of its muzzle.

Do wolf packs change?

Wolf packs are constantly changing. Sometimes, a pack forces out a sick, injured or old wolf that cannot hunt. They often let it follow behind and eat their leftovers. A young adult wolf usually leaves its parents' pack when it is about two years old. It may join with another single wolf to search for a new **territory**. They **mate** and have young and become the **alpha** pair of a new pack.

A young wolf, like this **female** Arctic wolf, may leave its parents' pack to find a mate. The pair may then have pups and form their own pack.

New alpha wolves

If an alpha wolf dies or gets too old to lead the pack, the remaining alpha may find a new partner from outside the pack. In some cases the most important **beta** wolf takes over. He or she then chooses an outside wolf for a partner and they become the alpha pair of the pack.

Do wolf packs fight?

There is very little fighting within a wolf pack, because everyone knows their place and the **rank** order helps to keep the peace. Fights can happen when a pack is very large, or when there is not enough food for everyone. Fights can end with a pack splitting into two, or in one wolf leaving the pack.

Instead of fighting, a dominant wolf usually crouches over a lower-ranking wolf, staring at it, baring its teeth and growling, like this. This warning is enough to stop trouble.

Fights with other packs

Just as wolves try to avoid fights within their packs, they also avoid fighting other wolf packs. The **scent marks** that wolves use to mark their pack's **territory** warn other wolves to keep away. This allows both sets of wolves to avoid a fight. Sometimes, though, when food is scarce, wolves stray into each other's territories in search of a meal.

Peacekeeping

Wolves can usually avoid fights by using body language. A dominant wolf may remind a lesser wolf that it has more power by staring hard at it or nipping its **muzzle**. A lower-ranking wolf shows it knows its place and does not want to fight by crouching down and flattening its ears.

The pack that owns the territory chases the intruders. If they do not clear off fast enough, the two packs can end up fighting. Fights between different wolf packs can be vicious and often end with some wolves from each side being injured or killed.

Wolves have strong bodies and sharp, powerful teeth for catching **prey**. These weapons can cause serious damage to other wolves when different wolf packs fight each other.

There are few animals that cause danger to wolves. This is one advantage of living in a group. It is much more dangerous for another animal to attack a wolf that is part of a pack than it would be to attack a wolf on its own. The only wild animals that really threaten wolves are pumas and bears. These animals don't hunt adult wolves to eat them, but may injure or kill wolves in fights over dead animals that one or the other has killed.

Pup problems

● ● ● ● ● ● ● ● ● ● ●

About half of the wolf pups born each year die before their first birthday. Many die from disease, fights or accidents. Grizzly bears sometimes dig up dens to eat the wolf pups left inside while their mothers are away.

Wolves fight bears that try to take their food or get near their den. These fights can be fierce and wolves are often killed.

A hard life

They may not have many **predators**, but wolves don't usually live past ten years old. They may be killed by disease, injuries or **parasites**. Wolves may be injured, or even killed, by large **prey** that defend themselves when wolves attack them.

Wolves and people

A wolf pack's main enemy is people. Today, wolves are an **endangered species** because people have hunted and killed so many of them. Some people kill wolves for their fur or because they fear wolves might attack them. People also kill wolves because they are a danger to farm animals, such as cattle and sheep, although wolves only catch farm animals when they cannot find wild prey.

Moose can kill wolves that attack them by kicking out with their heavy hooves or lunging at wolves with their antlers.

27

Territory troubles

People also harm wolf packs when they change the land that they live and hunt in. For example, when trees are cut down for wood or to clear land for farming or building, the deer that fed on the forest plants starve. Wolf packs living there lose their homes and their food – the deer – so they eventually die as well.

Protecting wolves

In many countries, laws stop people from hunting wolves, or limit the number they can kill. People who know about wolves are teaching others that there is no need to fear these animals because they avoid people. Happily, in some places, such as **national parks**, actions like these have led to an increase in the number of wolves living there.

In North America, wolves have not killed a single person for over 100 years. People, on the other hand, have killed thousands of wolves in that time.

Wolf facts

Where do wolves live?

Most of the world's grey wolves live in the map areas that are green.

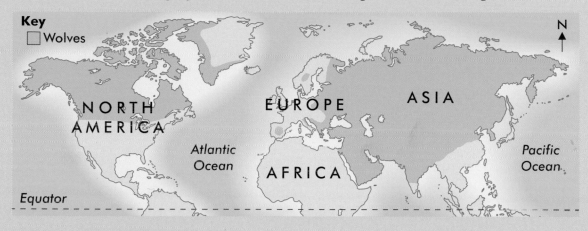

Fast and silent

Wolves run on their toes, holding the back parts of their feet off the ground. This allows them to move very quickly and quietly. They can keep up a fast-paced chase for about 20 minutes. Wolves are usually 1 to 1.5 metres long and they can leap up to 5 metres at a time.

Wolves and prey populations

Wolves usually catch the weakest, oldest or sickest animals in a herd. These animals are least likely to hurt the wolves and they are easiest to capture. The weakest animals in a herd of, say, deer, are likely to die anyway, but in the meantime they compete for food with the others. By killing them, the wolves actually help to maintain a healthy herd.

Wolf sayings

In the past people feared wolves. Many old sayings that mention wolves use them to mean something bad or evil. 'A wolf in sheep's clothing' describes someone who is pretending to be kind or good when really they are wicked. 'To keep the wolf from the door' means to prevent poverty or hunger.

Glossary

alpha   used to describe the dominant male or female wolf in a pack

ancestor   animal that lived in the past and from which others have evolved

beta   used to describe wolves that are below the alphas but above their brothers and sisters in the rank order

camouflage   colours and patterns that help an animal's body to blend in with its background

carrion   meat eaten from a dead animal that is found dead

communicate   pass on a message containing information to another animal or person

den   place where wolf pups are born and where they live until they are about two months old

dominant   leader, or most important member of a group

endangered species   any type of animal or plant that is in danger of becoming extinct (dying out)

female   animal that, when mature, can produce eggs that can be fertilized by a sperm. A female human is called a woman or girl.

habitat   place where an animal or plant lives

hibernate   go into a long and very deep sleep during cold weather

litter   young animals born at the same time to the same mother

male   animal that, when mature, can produce sperm that can fertilize female eggs. A male human is called a man or boy.

mate   what a male and female animal do to start a baby growing inside the female. An animal's mate is an animal of the other sex that they can have young with.

migrate   when animals move from one place to another far away

muzzle   nose and mouth of an animal from the dog family

national park   area of natural beauty that is protected by law, so that people cannot change or damage it

parasite   animal (or plant) that lives on or inside another living thing

predators   animals that hunt other animals for food

prey   animal that is hunted and eaten as food by another animal

rank   place in an order of things

scavenger   animal that steals food from other animals

scent mark   when an animal sprays strong smelling urine (wee) somewhere as a signal that they have been there

scent trail   smell that an animal leaves behind on the ground that other animals can follow

social   living in well-organized groups that work together

species   group of living things that are similar and can reproduce together to produce healthy offspring

stalk   sneak up on prey in order to get close enough to catch it

suckle   when a baby animal drinks its mother's milk

territory   particular area that an animal claims as its own, and which it defends against uninvited visitors

Find out more

Books

Our Wild World: Wolves, Laura Evert (Northwest Press, 2000)

Wild World: Wolves, Karen Dudley (A & C Black, 2001)

Wolves, Karen Wallace (Oxford University Press, 2000)

Crafty Canines: Coyotes, Foxes and Wolves, Phyllis J. Perry (Franklin Watts, 2000)

Websites

www.bbc.co.uk/nature/wildfacts

www.geocities.com

www.nationalgeographic.com/geoguide/wolves

www.exzooberance.com

(Also has pictures you can download for free.)

Index

Titles in the *Animal Groups* series include:

Hardback   0 431 16922 5

Hardback   0 431 16920 9

Hardback   0 431 16925 X

Hardback   0 431 16923 3

Hardback   0 431 16921 7

Hardback   0 431 16924 1

Find out about the other titles in this series on our website www.heinemann.co.uk/library